AF228912

TIME TRAVEL

IS VISITING THE PAST AND FUTURE POSSIBLE?

MEGAN BORGERT-SPANIOL

Checkerboard
Library

An Imprint of Abdo Publishing
abdopublishing.com

Published by Abdo Publishing, a division of ABDO, PO Box 398166, Minneapolis, Minnesota 55439.
Copyright © 2019 by Abdo Consulting Group, Inc. International copyrights reserved in all countries.
No part of this book may be reproduced in any form without written permission from the publisher.
Checkerboard Library™ is a trademark and logo of Abdo Publishing.

Printed in China
052018
092018

Design: Emily O'Malley, Mighty Media, Inc.
Production: Mighty Media, Inc.
Editor: Jessie Alkire
Cover Photographs: Shutterstock
Interior Photographs: Alamy, p. 19; AP Images, pp. 23, 27; Clemens Vasters/Flickr, p. 20; Library of
Congress, p. 5; Lwp Kommunikáció/Flickr, p. 24; National Archives and Records Administration, pp. 17,
28 (bottom left); Shutterstock, pp. 14, 28 (bottom right); sv1ambo/Flickr, pp. 13, 29 (bottom); Wikimedia
Commons, pp. 7, 9, 10, 28 (top), 29 (top)

Library of Congress Control Number: 2017961635

Publisher's Cataloging-in-Publication Data
Names: Borgert-Spaniol, Megan, author.
Title: Time travel: Is visiting the past and future possible? / by Megan Borgert-Spaniol.
Other titles: Is visiting the past and future possible?
Description: Minneapolis, Minnesota : Abdo Publishing, 2019. | Series: Science fact or
   science fiction? | Includes online resources and index.
Identifiers: ISBN 9781532115417 (lib.bdg.) | ISBN 9781532156137 (ebook)
Subjects: LCSH: Time travel--Juvenile literature. | Space and time--Juvenile literature. |
   Answers to questions--Juvenile literature. | Science fiction in science education—
   Juvenile literature.
Classification: DDC 530.11--dc23

CONTENTS

It was a cold morning on November 19, 1863. Thousands of people were gathered in Gettysburg, Pennsylvania. They had come to hear President Lincoln deliver what would become his famous Gettysburg Address.

Ten-year-old Andrew Basiago was among the crowd. Andrew had dressed as a **bugle boy** to blend in with other boys at the event. But he had lost his shoes during his journey to Gettysburg. Now, he was wearing a borrowed pair of men's shoes.

Andrew felt that his oversized shoes were attracting attention. He decided to step away from the gathered crowd. He clutched a letter addressed to the Secretary of the Navy, Gideon Welles. In it, Andrew asked Welles to help him if he was arrested. Andrew did not belong in the year 1863. In fact, he had come from more than 100 years in the future!

Now an adult, Basiago has shared this story with the public since 2004. For evidence, he points to a photo

The Gettysburg Address is one of the most well-known speeches in US history. Lincoln spoke about equality and freedom in the face of the Civil War.

taken at the Gettysburg Address. The photo shows a young boy in big shoes standing apart from the crowd. Basiago claims the boy is his younger self! Did Basiago really travel through time?

Time travel is the movement backward or forward between two points in time. The idea might seem simple at first. But time travel exists in several different **contexts**.

The most popular context for time travel is science fiction. Since the late 1800s, writers have explored the idea of human travel into the past or future. These writers invent their own **logic**, **technology**, and consequences of time travel. They are free to imagine time travel without being limited by what is currently possible.

Time travel stories also exist in the real world. Basiago is one of many people who have claimed to travel into the past or future. Some of these people have claimed to do so with the help of technologies such as time machines. Many others have claimed to suddenly slip through **portals** in space and time without trying to do so.

Time travel is also a topic of scientific study. This idea of time travel is different from the kind shown in fiction

The TV series *Star Trek* had many episodes that involved time travel. It introduced many viewers to new concepts about time travel.

and personal accounts. It exists mainly in theory or on a very small scale.

Scientific theories of time travel can be difficult to understand. Meanwhile, real-life claims of time travel can be convincing. This leaves many people searching for answers. Are humans capable of time travel? Is visiting the past and future possible?

Time travel has been a topic of human interest for thousands of years. It was mentioned around the 400s BCE in the ancient Indian text *Mahabharata*. In it, a king travels to heaven and then back to Earth. Upon his return, the king learns that many years have passed.

But it wasn't until the 1800s that time travel became a popular idea in science fiction. The **Industrial Revolution** saw great advances in **technology** and science. People began to dream of what the future might hold. One of those people was English writer H.G. Wells.

In 1895, Wells published a book called *The Time Machine*. It tells the story of an inventor who builds a machine for traveling through time. He then uses the machine to travel thousands of years into the future.

The Time Machine was the first work of fiction to imagine time travel in this way. It inspired people to dream of how time travel might work. It made people wonder what could happen if time travel was achieved.

H.G. Wells wrote several influential science-fiction books, as well as many short stories, essays, and nonfiction books.

Albert Einstein went on to receive the Nobel Prize in Physics in 1921 for his work in theoretical physics.

Not long after *The Time Machine* was published, **physicist** Albert Einstein began exploring similar ideas. In 1905, Einstein introduced his theory that space and time are connected. He believed that time slows down or speeds up depending on how quickly one moves through space. Theories like Einstein's inspired science-fiction writers to explore time travel in depth.

Throughout the 1900s, stories featuring time travel amazed readers and audiences. As the subject grew in popularity, real reports of time travel became common. Some people claimed to witness time travelers. Others shared stories of their own journeys into the past or future.

As science and **technology** have advanced, more researchers have taken interest in the study of time. In 1995, **physicist** David Anderson formed the Time Travel Research Center in New York. There, he led research on controlling time and developing time travel technologies. Anderson claimed that time travel would one day be possible.

Many scientists have rejected such claims. They say human time travel is impossible. But reports of time travel continue to attract attention around the world. To many people, time travel is not just a possibility. It is a reality!

Some of the most famous cases of time travel have come from the minds of science-fiction writers. Many books and short stories have **chronicled** a character's travels to a single point in history. These stories often present possible consequences of traveling into the past. American writer Ray Bradbury explored this theme in a 1952 short story called "A Sound of Thunder."

Bradbury's story begins in the year 2055. A man travels back to prehistoric times to hunt dinosaurs. When he returns to the future, the world isn't quite the same as he left it. Then, the man finds a crushed butterfly on his boot. He had accidentally stepped on it during his prehistoric adventure. This small action sparked a series of events that changed how the future unfolded.

FOR REAL?

In 1985, *Back to the Future* earned more than $381 million in ticket sales. It was the highest-earning movie of the whole year!

The 1985 movie *Back to the Future* teaches a similar lesson. The main character, Marty McFly, travels back to 1955. There, he accidentally prevents his parents from meeting each other. He then must find a way to get his parents to meet. If they don't meet, Marty will cease to exist!

In *Back to the Future*, Marty McFly travels through time in a time machine made from a DeLorean car!

Bold Street was built on sandstone. Some people believe the mineral quartz in sandstone could create a magnetic field that causes time slips!

Time travel to the past has reportedly occurred in real life too. Many people have claimed to slip briefly from the present to the past while physically remaining in the same location. These experiences are known as "time slips."

In 1901, two professors from England reported such a time slip during a visit to France. Anne Moberly and Eleanor Jourdain were walking the grounds of the Palace of Versailles. Suddenly, they came upon a group of people dressed in 1780s-style clothing. Among the group was Marie Antoinette, the former queen of France. Moberly and Jourdain were shocked. Antoinette had been executed more than 100 years earlier!

Reports of similar time slips have occurred on Bold Street in Liverpool, England. One incident occurred in 1996. A man was crossing the street when he suddenly noticed his surroundings had changed. Cars looked old-fashioned. People were dressed in 1950s-style clothing. The man looked up to see a clothing store he had never heard of. When he walked into the store, he found himself back in the present!

One widely reported claim of time travel to the past involves the US government. Basiago's story about the Gettysburg Address is just one of his time travel experiences. Basiago has said that he was involved in the US government's "Project Pegasus" as a child. He participated in the program from 1968 to 1972. The program researched time travel and its effects on kids.

Basiago reportedly made several trips through time. Basiago said he used several different time travel **technologies**. He described one machine as a curtain of **radiant** energy. This energy is said to bend space and time. Basiago said participants jumped through the curtain to travel to different times and locations.

Basiago recounts his time travels and the science behind them in great detail. He points to the photo taken at the Gettysburg Address as evidence of his journeys to the past. Basiago has convinced many people that the US government holds the secrets to time travel!

Name:

- Basiago, Andrew

Born:

- September 18, 1961, Morristown, New Jersey

Claims:

- Participated in "Project Pegasus" as a child
- Traveled to the past using several different time travel **technologies**
- Witnessed President Lincoln's 1863 Gettysburg Address
- Was present at Ford's Theatre during 1865 Lincoln **Assassination**

Evidence:

- Detailed accounts of time travel and the technologies used
- Photo of a boy standing apart from the crowd at 1863 Gettysburg Address

Status:

UNPROVEN

In science fiction, traveling to the past allows humans to experience or even change history. Traveling to the future provides a glimpse of what the world will or could be like. Wells's *The Time Machine* is one example of this.

In the story, a time traveler visits the year 802,701. He encounters what looks like a peaceful society. He later learns its darker secrets. Wells used his story to comment on the English class system of the late 1800s. He also explored the science of traveling through time with a machine.

Real claims of travel to the future have little in common with *The Time Machine*. They involve smaller leaps in time. And they usually involve **involuntary** time slips instead of traveling with time machines.

One famous time slip into the future was said to occur in 1935. Air Marshal Sir Robert Victor Goddard was flying his plane from Scotland to England. On his way, he flew over an abandoned airfield outside Edinburgh, Scotland.

Soon after, he flew into a storm. He made his way back to
the airfield to wait out the storm.

As Goddard approached the airfield, the clouds cleared. The sun was shining. And the airfield was no longer abandoned. There were mechanics in blue jumpsuits. There were unfamiliar yellow planes. Goddard was **perplexed**. Was this the same abandoned airfield he had just flown over?

A possible explanation of the scene came four years later. The British Royal Air Force started painting their training planes yellow. Its mechanics switched from brown to blue jumpsuits. Had Goddard flown briefly into the future during his 1935 flight?

Another time slip to the future reportedly took place in Louisiana in 1969. Two men were driving along a highway when they approached an old-fashioned car. The woman driving the car was wearing 1940s-style clothing. She looked scared and confused.

The men motioned to the woman to pull over so they could help her. Then they pulled onto the side of the road. But when they looked around, the old car was nowhere to be found. Had the men witnessed a person from the past slip into the future?

Real claims of time travel are thought by many to be made-up stories. However, most **physicists** believe that time travel is possible in theory. Einstein presented his theories on space and time more than 100 years ago. Today, time travel science is still rooted in these theories.

One theory that allows for time travel is called time dilation. This theory says that time moves more slowly for anything moving near the speed of light. The speed of light is how fast light waves move.

To understand this theory, imagine a spaceship leaving Earth near the speed of light. At this speed, time on the spaceship moves more slowly than time on Earth. So, a person on the spaceship ages more slowly than humans back on Earth.

FOR REAL?

Astronauts cannot travel near the speed of light. But they experience a small degree of time dilation when they travel into space. In effect, they return to Earth fractions of a second in the future!

The idea that nothing moves faster than light is represented in Einstein's theory of relativity. This is the famous $E=mc^2$ equation, where energy equals mass times the speed of light squared.

Now imagine the spaceship returns to Earth after a year of travel. On Earth, about three years have passed. In effect, the spaceship has traveled into the future when it returns to Earth!

In 2009, physicist Stephen Hawking hosted a party for time travelers. He sent invitations after the party took place, so he'd know if the guests were from the future. But no one showed up!

Time dilation is a widely accepted theory. It has been demonstrated in many experiments using tiny particles. Because of this, most **physicists** support the idea that time travel to the future is possible. But not all scientists believe in time travel to the past. Experts say this would require that humans travel faster than the speed of light. This is considered impossible by most scientists.

Another route for travel to the past is through passages called "wormholes." A wormhole is thought of as a bridge or **shortcut** between two points in space and time. Some people believe such shortcuts could allow for travel to the past or future.

Einstein's theories provide support for the existence of wormholes. However, scientists have not yet observed a wormhole. **Physicists** can only **hypothesize** about whether wormholes are real and how they might work.

Time travel to the past also raises questions of **logic**. Imagine that, like Marty McFly, you traveled to the past and stopped your parents from meeting. This would prevent you from ever being born. So, you wouldn't have been able to go back in time in the first place.

There are theories that work around this **paradox**. One theory says the laws of physics would prevent you from changing the past. Another theory says that going back in time creates multiple timelines. Say you stopped your parents from meeting. You would still exist in your original timeline. But you would also create a parallel universe in which you were never born!

Experiments have shown that time travel is possible on a small scale. But this has only been demonstrated using tiny particles. More significant time travel, like moving days or years into the future, is a different matter. **Technology** to move a human near the speed of light doesn't exist yet. It would also take huge amounts of energy to do so. Finally, experts don't think the human body could survive traveling near the speed of light.

Still, researchers have studied the math behind the speed of light. In 2012, mathematicians James Hill and Barry Cox published a paper on the subject. Hill and Cox argued that traveling at the speed of light could be mathematically possible.

They compared speed of light travel to speed of sound travel. Earlier researchers believed traveling faster than the speed of sound was impossible, yet Chuck Yeager did so in 1947. Hill and Cox question if doubts about traveling faster than the speed of light could be incorrect too.

The Large Hadron Collider (LHC) is a machine that speeds up particles. Some researchers think the LHC could speed certain particles enough to travel backward or forward in time.

Will time travel become possible in the future? Or have some humans already discovered its secrets? Advances in science and **technology** may one day provide an answer. It is only a matter of time!

TIMELINE

400s BCE
Time travel is mentioned in the ancient Indian text *Mahabharata*.

1895
H.G. Wells publishes *The Time Machine*.

1901
Two professors report seeing long-dead Marie Antoinette during a trip to France.

1905
Physicist Albert Einstein introduces the theory that space and time are connected.

1935
Air Marshal Sir Robert Victor Goddard experiences what may be a time slip into the future in Scotland.

1985
The movie *Back to the Future* explores the consequences of traveling to the past.

1995
Physicist David Anderson forms the Time Travel Research Center.

1996
A man in Liverpool, England claims to experience a time slip on Bold Street.

2004
Andrew Basiago claims to have participated in government research on time travel when he was a child.

2012
Researchers James Hill and Barry Cox publish a paper on the math behind the speed of light.

YOU DECIDE!

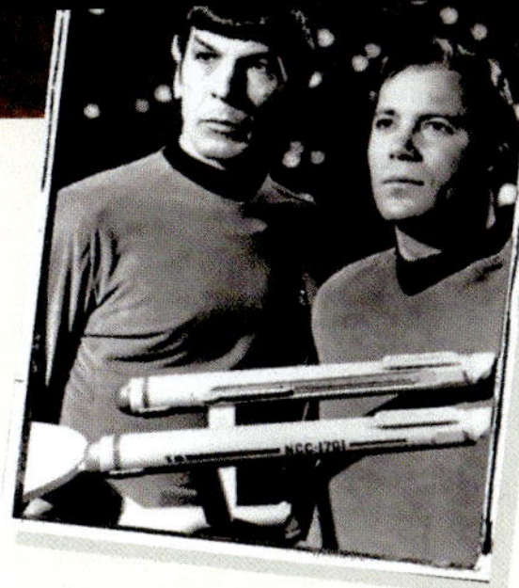

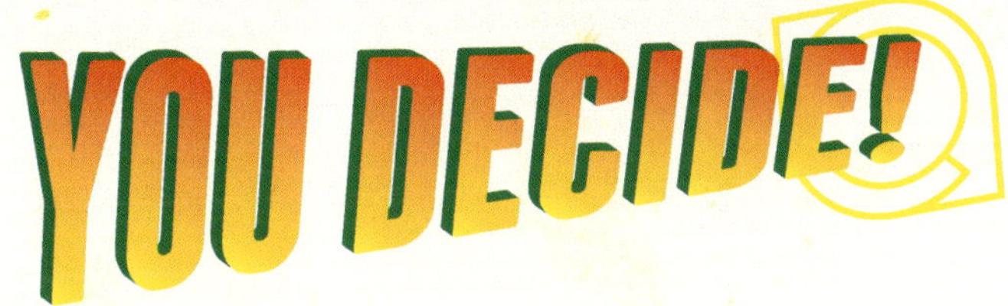

Is visiting the past and future possible? You decide!

- Explore time travel in science-fiction books and movies.
- Research real claims of time travel online.
- Read articles about time dilation, wormholes, and other theories of time travel.
- Look out for evidence of time slips and time travelers from the future!

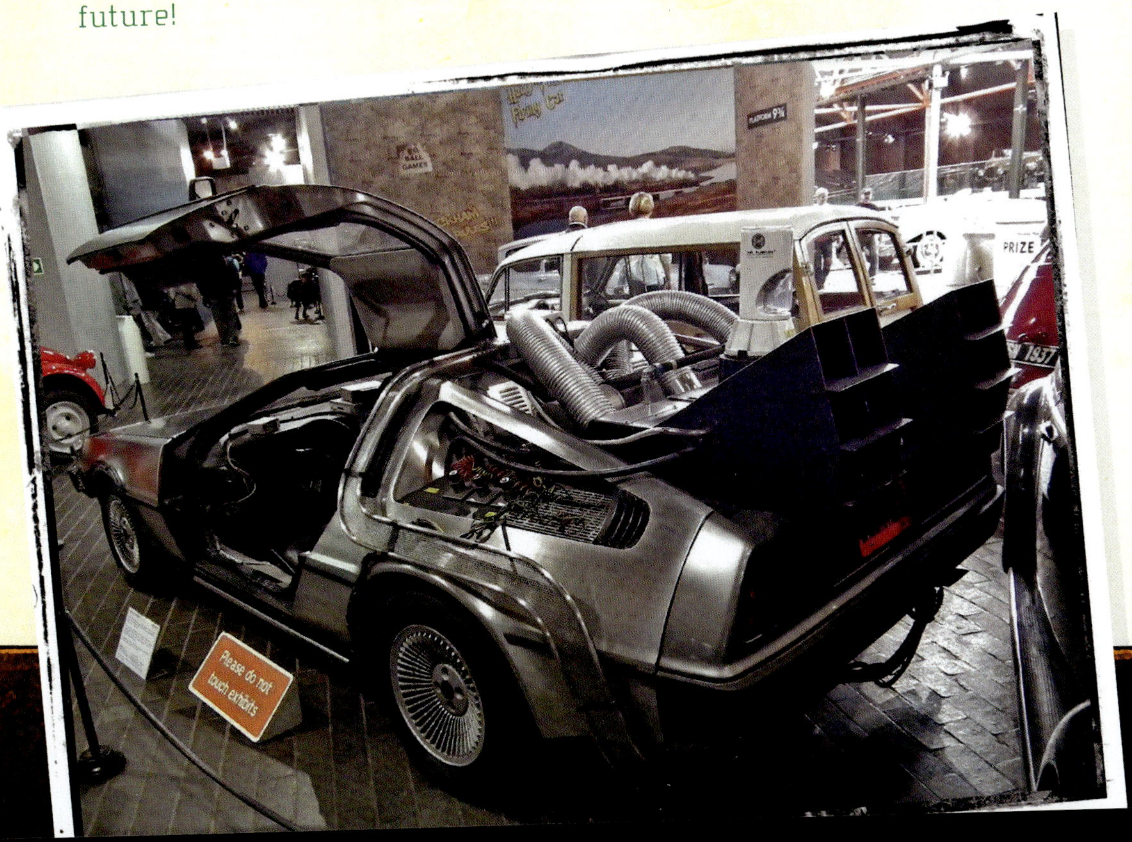

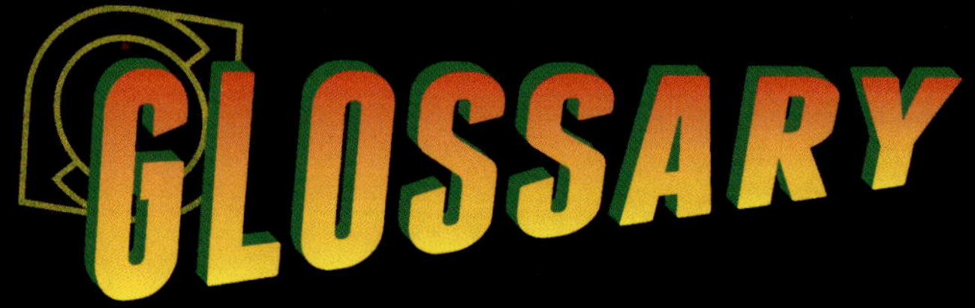

GLOSSARY

assassination—the murder of a very important person, usually for political reasons.

bugle boy—someone who plays a bugle, a brass instrument, usually in the military.

chronicle—to describe an event.

context—the circumstances that form the setting or understanding for an event or idea.

hypothesize—to make a hypothesis, or guess, based on a set of facts.

Industrial Revolution—a period in the United States and Europe from about 1750 to 1850. It marked the change from an agricultural to an industrial society.

involuntary—not done willingly or by choice.

landmark—a feature, such as a building, that is well-known and can be seen from far away.

logic—sensible thinking or reasoning.

paradox—something that seems to be both possible and impossible.

perplexed—baffled or puzzled.

physics—the science of how energy and objects affect each other. Someone who studies physics is a physicist.

portal—an entrance.

radiant—transmitted by radiation.

shortcut—a shorter or easier way.

tattoo—a design on the body made using a needle to put color under the skin.

technology—scientific tools or methods for doing tasks or solving problems.

ONLINE RESOURCES

To learn more about time travel, visit **abdobooklinks.com**. These links are routinely monitored and updated to provide the most current information available.

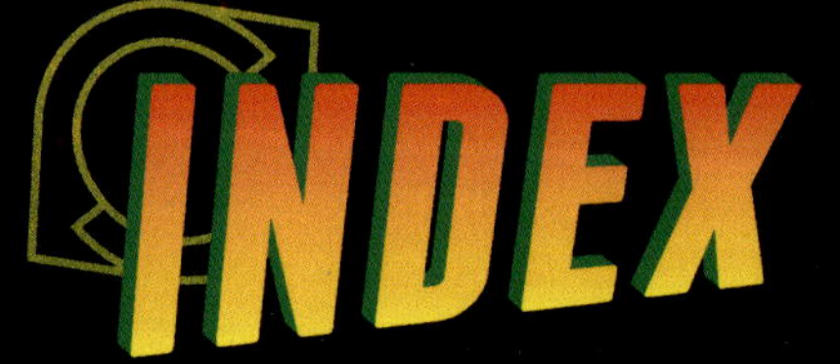

INDEX